DATE DUE			

7029

612
BER

Berger, Melvin.

Why I cough, sneeze, shiver, hiccup, & yawn

Why I Cough, Sneeze, Shiver, Hiccup, & Yawn

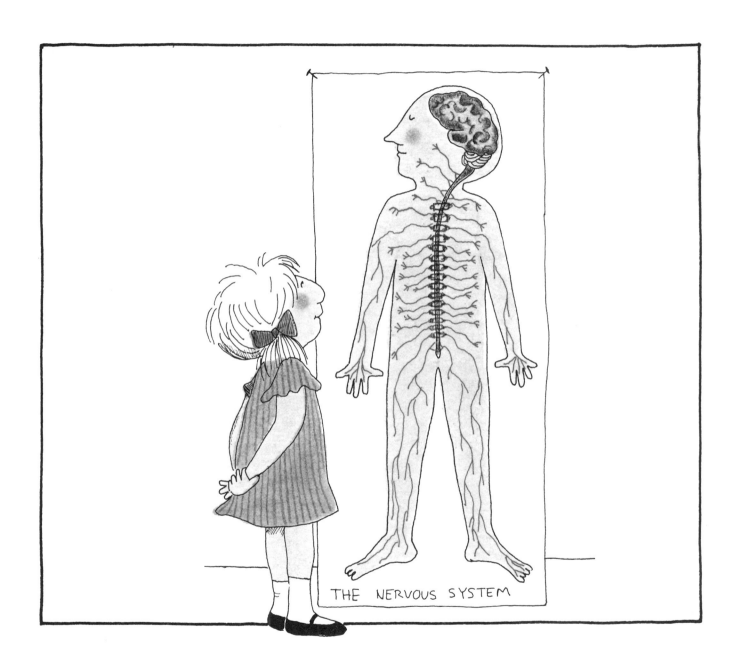

THE NERVOUS SYSTEM

This Is a Let's-Read-and-Find-Out Science Book®

Why I Cough, Sneeze, Shiver, Hiccup, & Yawn

by Melvin Berger

illustrated by Holly Keller

HarperCollinsPublishers

Other Recent Let's-Read-and-Find-Out Science Books® You Will Enjoy

The *Let's-Read-and-Find-Out Science Book* series was originated by Dr. Franklyn M. Branley, Astronomer Emeritus and former Chairman of the American Museum–Hayden Planetarium, and was formerly co-edited by him and Dr. Roma Gans, Professor Emeritus of Childhood Education, Teachers College, Columbia University. For a complete catalog of Let's-Read-and-Find-Out Science Books, write to HarperCollins Children's Books, 10 East 53rd Street, New York, NY 10022.

Library of Congress Cataloging-in-Publication Data
Berger, Melvin.
    Why I cough, sneeze, shiver, hiccup, and yawn.
    (Let's-read-and-find-out science book)
    Summary: An introduction to reflex acts that explains why we cough, sneeze, shiver, hiccup, yawn, and blink.
    1. Reflexes—Juvenile literature. [1. Reflexes]
I. Keller, Holly. II. Title. III. Series.
PQ372.B3964   1983   612′.74   82-45587
ISBN 0-690-04253-1.—ISBN 0-690-04254-X (lib. bdg.)

Designed by Ellen Weiss
8 9 10

You are playing hide and seek. You've found a good hiding place. You want to be as quiet as you can. All of a sudden—KA-CHOO! You sneeze. Everyone knows where you are.

Why do you sneeze—even when you don't want to?

You are taking a nice warm bath. It's time to get out of the tub. As you step out, you feel cold. B-R-R-R! You start to shiver. Your whole body shakes.

Why do you shiver—even when you don't want to?

You are eating lunch with your friends. You are in the middle of telling them a story. All at once you hiccup. HIC! Your friends start to laugh. HIC! You try to stop. HIC! But you can't. HIC!

Why do you hiccup—even when you don't want to?

A sneeze is a reflex. Shivers and hiccups are reflexes, too. You don't have to think about making them happen. Reflexes happen whether you want them to or not. They happen very fast, and it is hard to stop them.

All reflexes work through your nervous system.

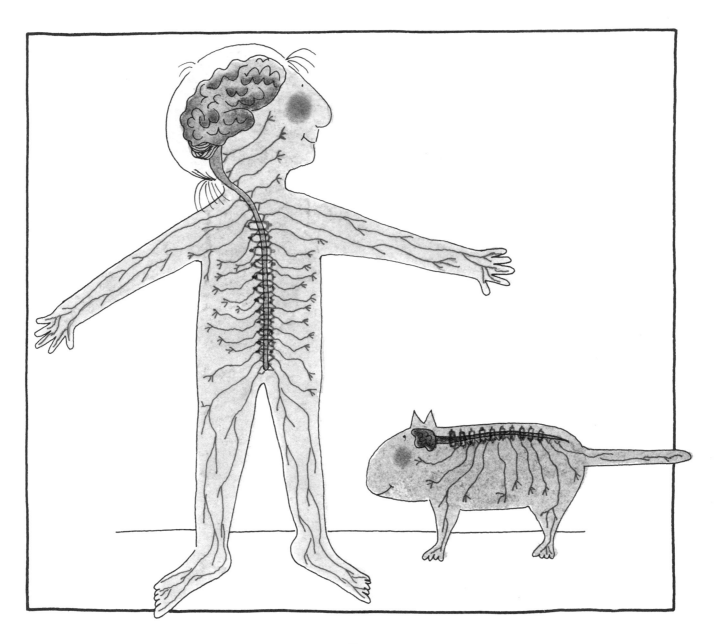

Your nervous system is made up of two parts.
One part is the nerves. The nerves look like long,
thin threads. They reach all over your body.

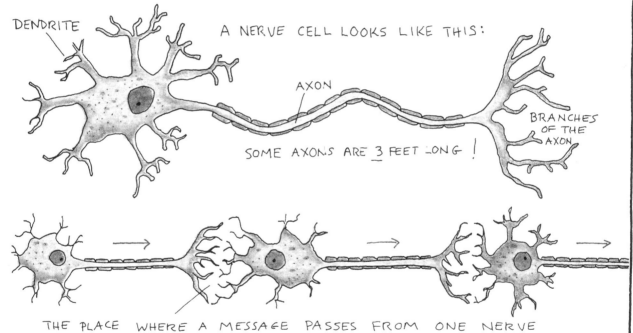

DENDRITE

A NERVE CELL LOOKS LIKE THIS:

AXON

BRANCHES OF THE AXON

SOME AXONS ARE 3 FEET LONG !

THE PLACE WHERE A MESSAGE PASSES FROM ONE NERVE CELL TO ANOTHER IS CALLED A SYNAPSE.

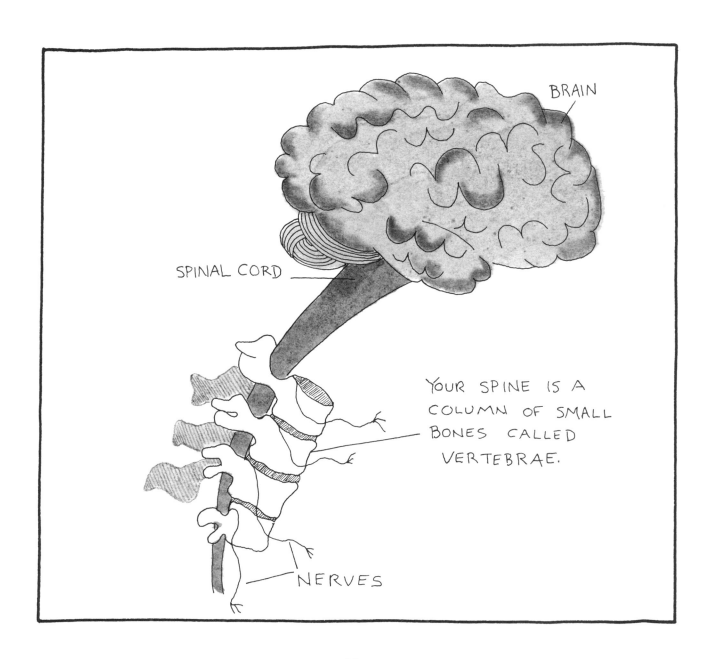

BRAIN

SPINAL CORD

YOUR SPINE IS A
COLUMN OF SMALL
BONES CALLED
VERTEBRAE.

NERVES

The other part is the spinal cord and brain. The spinal cord is a thick bundle of nerves. It is inside your spine, or backbone. The brain is at the upper end of the spinal cord. It is made up of billions of tiny nerves.

Nerves are like telephone wires. They carry messages back and forth. The brain and spinal cord are like the main office of the telephone company. All the messages must go through here.

Suppose you put your finger on a hot stove. The nerves in your hand sense that the stove is hot. They send out a message.

The message speeds along nerves from your hand to your spinal cord. Here the message passes to a different nerve. This nerve controls the muscles that move your arm.

A signal flashes through this nerve. It tells your muscles to move your hand—and fast. Before you even know it hurts, your hand jerks away from the stove.

Pulling your hand off a hot stove is a reflex act. It happens very quickly, and it is not completely under your control. It happens automatically, without your having to think about making it happen.

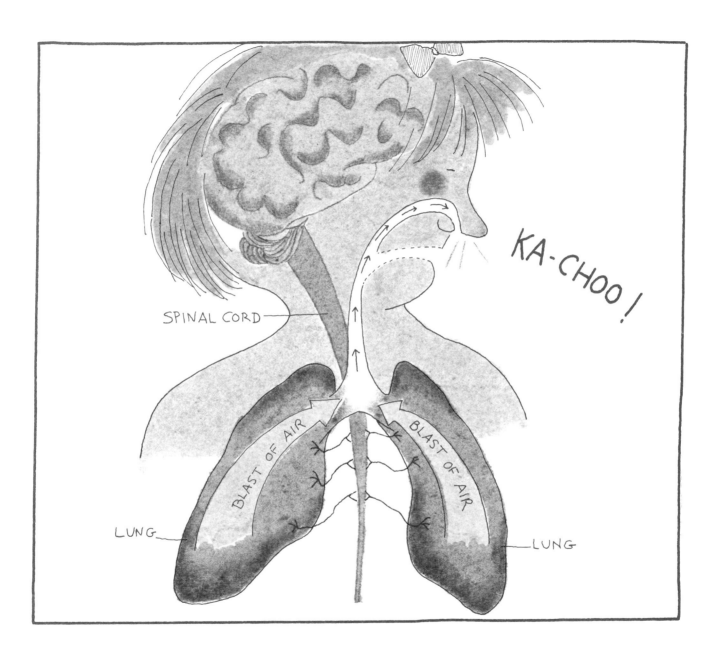

A sneeze is also a reflex. A bit of dust or dirt gets into your nose. The nerves sense that something is there that is not supposed to be. They shoot the message to the spinal cord and brain.

In the spinal cord, the message passes to other nerves that go to your lungs. These nerves tell your lungs to send up a blast of air. KA-CHOO! You sneeze. The sneeze blows the dust or dirt out of your nose.

A sneeze is a reflex that protects you. Sneezing helps to blow dust and dirt and other irritating substances out of your nose.

This is why you shiver. You step out of a warm bath into a cool room. The nerves in your skin feel that it is cold in the room. They carry the message to nerves in your spinal cord.

From the spinal cord the message races through other nerves. All over your body, muscles quickly tighten and loosen, tighten and loosen. You are shivering. The moving muscles produce heat. The shivers warm you up.

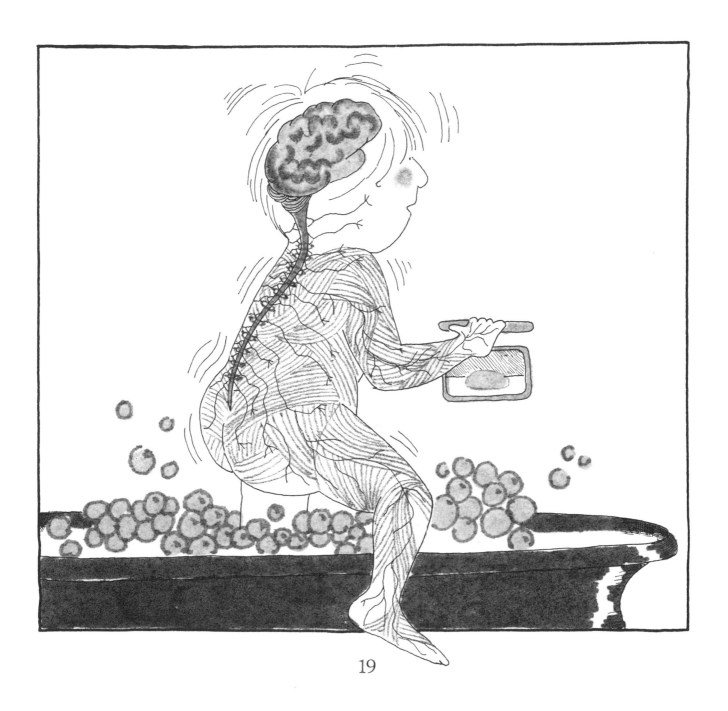

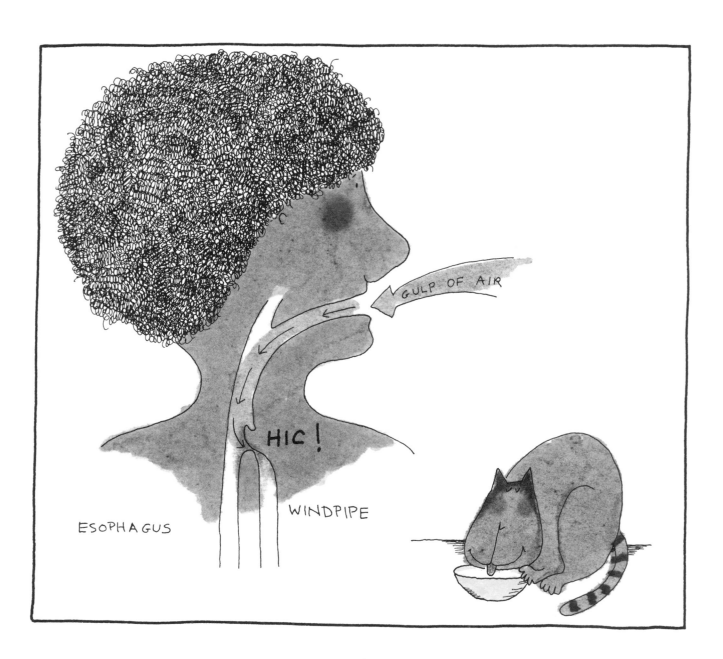

No one knows exactly why hiccups happen. We do know how they work. A message races to your spinal cord. From there a nerve sends out a signal that makes you take in a big gulp of air. But at that moment your throat closes. The air bumps against your closed throat. It makes a sound—HIC! It is a hiccup. The sound gives the hiccup its name.

The hiccup is a reflex. A drink of water may make the hiccups go away.

Have you ever tried to hold back a yawn? It is very hard to do. A yawn is another reflex.

A yawn begins when the lungs have too little oxygen in them. Nerves signal the muscles around your jaw to pull apart. You yawn, and as you do, you take an extra-deep breath of air. With more oxygen in your lungs, you feel a little less sleepy.

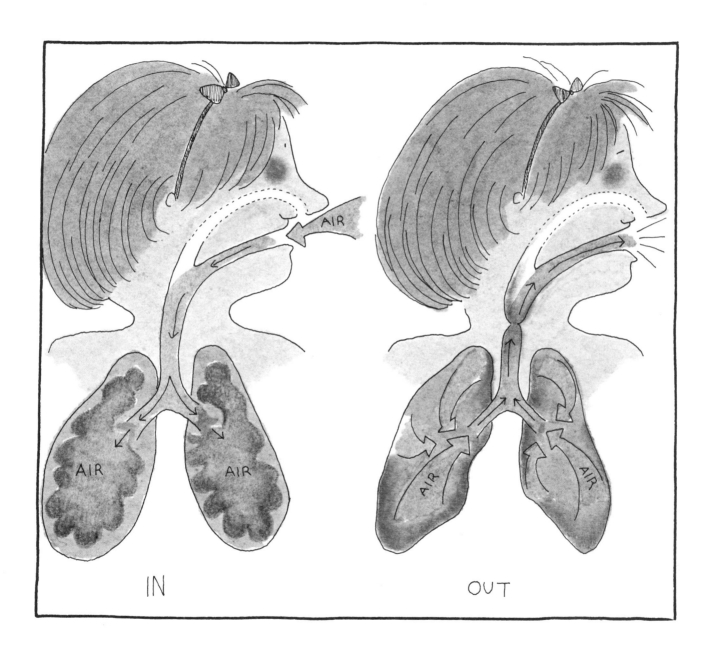

IN   OUT

A cough can be a reflex, too. When you have a cold, substances in your throat sometimes irritate the nerves. The nerves send out a message. You gulp in air.

Meanwhile, your throat closes partway, so the air is trapped inside your lungs. Suddenly there is too much pressure. The air explodes out. The cough clears the irritation out of your throat.

What happens when food gets stuck in your throat? You cough then, too. Coughing frees the food. It clears your throat. It saves you from choking.

A reflex you can see happens in your eyes. Close your eyes and keep them closed for a few minutes. Then look in a mirror. The black part of your eye—that's the pupil—will be big and round.

A reflex makes the pupils in your eyes grow larger when there is too little light. It makes the pupils grow smaller in bright light. You can see it happen.

Doctors sometimes test reflexes. Have you ever had the test? You sit on a table with your legs hanging down. The doctor taps your leg just below the knee. The tool that is used looks like a hammer with a rubber head.

Suddenly your leg kicks up. This is a reflex. It is sometimes called the patellar reflex, or knee jerk. A strong patellar reflex is usually a sign of a healthy nervous system.

Here is a reflex that you can test for yourself. Take off a shoe and sock. Ask a friend to gently scratch the bottom of your foot with a toothpick. The scratch should go from your heel to your big toe.

Watch your toes slowly bend down. This is called the plantar reflex. It probably helps people walk on rough ground or climb trees with bare feet.

You have dozens of different reflexes. They protect your nose and throat from dust and dirt. They can keep you from burning yourself on a hot stove. They warm you up when you feel cold.

Think of that the next time you sneeze when you don't want to—or when you cough, shiver, hiccup or yawn.

Melvin Berger is the author of nearly one hundred books for young readers, several of which have been named Outstanding Science Trade Books for Children by the National Science Teachers Association and the Children's Book Council. He has written three other Let's-Read-and-Find-Out Science Books: ENERGY FROM THE SUN; GERMS MAKE ME SICK! (a Reading Rainbow Book); and WHY I COUGH, SNEEZE, SHIVER, HICCUP, & YAWN.

A member of the New York Academy of Sciences, Mr. Berger lives in Great Neck, New York, with his wife, who is also a writer.

Holly Keller was born in New York City, was graduated from Sarah Lawrence College, and received her M.A. from Columbia University. She is the author and illustrator of many picture books, including GOODBYE, MAX and GERALDINE'S BIG SNOW. Ms. Keller has illustrated a number of books in the Let's-Read-and-Find-Out series, including AIR IS ALL AROUND YOU, SNOW IS FALLING, and SNAKES ARE HUNTERS.